The Inuit

Ivory Carvers of the Far North

Revised Edition

by Rachel A. Koestler-Grack

Consultant:
Rick Juliani, M.A.
Educator and Curriculum Coordinator
Hopi Day School
Kykotsmovi, Arizona

T0050897

CAPSTONE PRESS
a capstone imprint

Blue Earth Books are published by Capstone Press
1710 Roe Crest Drive, North Mankato, Minnesota 56003
www.mycapstone.com

Library of Congress Cataloging-in-Publication Data is available on the Library of Congress website.
ISBN: 978-1-5157-4215-9 (paperback)
ISBN: 978-1-5157-4378-1 (eBook PDF)

Editorial credits
Editor: Megan Schoeneberger
Series Designer: Kia Adams
Cover Production Designer: Jennifer Schonborn
Photo Researcher: Wanda Winch
Product Planning Editor: Karen Risch

Photo credits
Alamy: Heritage Image Partnership Ltd, 10, left 11, John Sylvester, 18, Ton Koene/VWPics, 20; Capstone Press: Gary Sundermeyer, 3, 9, 13, 27; Corbis: Gunter Marx Photography, 28, 29; Getty Images: Bettmann, left 26, Buyenlarge, right 23, De Agostini Picture Library, left 22, 24, 25, Dorling Kindersley, cover, George Holton, bottom right 7, Peter Harholdt, left 8, right 22, Print Collector, right 8, Sissie Brimberg, left 12, Universal History Archive, left 15, Werner Forman, right 15, Yvette Cardozo, 21; Granger: NYC, 6, 7, right 12, National Geographic Stock: Vintage Collection, 10, 11; Minden Pictures: Jim Brandenburg, right 29; Newscom: CM Dixon Heritage Images, right 26, Werner Forman Archive Heritage Images, left 23; North Wind Picture Archives, 4-5, 17; Wikimedia: Ansgar Walk, bottom right 25

Printed in the United States of America.
003663

Contents

Features

Try blueberry-topped snowcream with the recipe on page 9.

Make a soap carving on page 13.

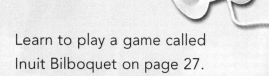

Learn to play a game called Inuit Bilboquet on page 27.

Chapter One

Winter in the Far North

Thousands of years ago, the Inuit people lived farther north than anyone else in the world. In the Arctic north, the sun did not rise during the long winter. For many months, only the moon and stars lit the icy land.

To pass time in the long winter, the Inuit made carvings. At first, they carved small tools from stone. Later, they collected the long, ivory teeth from walruses. They also saved animal bones and antlers from large deer called caribou. The Inuit carefully carved tiny shapes of men, women, and animals.

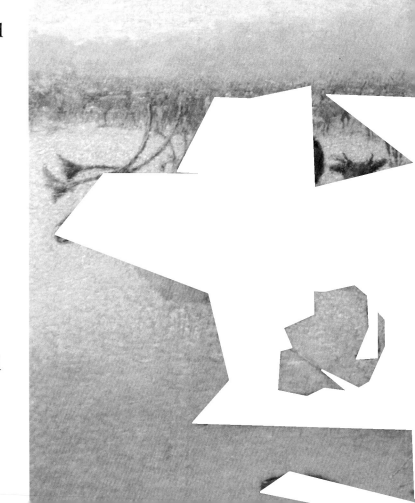

The Inuit Name

In the Inuit language, the Inuit name means "the real people."

But their far-off neighbors had a different name for them. The Inuit's only neighbors lived to the south in what is now Canada. Among their neighbors were their traditional enemies, the Cree Indians. The Cree called the Inuit "Eskimo." The name means "snowshoe netter." Today, the Inuit do not like to use that name.

The Inuit also used animals to help them move. Reindeer sometimes pulled their sleds.

5

Chapter Two

The Search for Food

Snow covered most of the Arctic all year. The land was too frozen and the air was too cold for the Inuit to grow food. Instead, they hunted animals for food.

Inuit men hunted whales with boats made of wood and animal skins. These boats were called kayaks. To search for a whale, the hunter paddled his boat between ice chunks floating in the water. When he spotted a whale, he used a long spear to kill it. After a few days, the dead whale washed up on shore. The Inuit then saved the whale meat on ice to keep it fresh.

An Inuit hunter used a long spear when hunting.

Inuit Homes

The Inuit often traveled to find food. On hunting trips, they built snow houses called igloos. The Inuit cut blocks of hard snow. They stacked the heavy blocks to make a dome. A skilled Inuit builder could make a small igloo in less than half an hour.

The Inuit did not always live in snow houses. They lived in earthen homes for much of the year. In summer, when the sun lit the sky all day and all night, some land thawed. The Inuit cut blocks of dirt from the ground. They stacked the blocks to build a home that lasted all year. On summer hunting trips, the Inuit sometimes lived in tents made with whale bones and caribou skin.

The Inuit built igloos by stacking blocks of snow.

The Inuit also hunted other animals. To kill seals, hunters waited by holes in the sea ice. When seals came to the holes to breathe, the hunters speared them. The Inuit used traps to catch polar bears and foxes. They hunted walrus and caribou with spears or bows and arrows. They also caught fish.

Inuit women and children also helped find food. During summer, they gathered bird eggs, seaweed, and fresh berries.

An Inuit hunter stood ready to spear seals that came to breathe at small holes in the ice.

Wooden serving trays held food for Inuit meals.

Blueberry-topped Snowcream

Inuit people ate mostly raw meat that was dried or frozen. But in late summer, women and children picked blueberries and bearberries. These berries were a tasty addition to their meals. You can make a simple dessert similar to the treats the Inuit enjoyed.

What You Need

Ingredients

½ cup (120 mL) fresh, clean blueberries

1 tablespoon (15 mL) sugar

About 6 ice cubes to make 1 cup (240 mL) crushed ice

Equipment

small bowl

dry-ingredient measuring cups

measuring spoons

spoon

serving dish

blender or food processor

What You Do

1. In small bowl, use a spoon to mix blueberries with sugar. Chill in refrigerator for 10 minutes.
2. Place serving dish in freezer to chill.
3. In a blender or food processor, crush ice into a snowlike consistency.
4. Remove serving dish from freezer. Spoon crushed ice into chilled dish. Top with the blueberry and sugar mixture.

Makes 1 serving

9

Chapter Three

More than Meat

The Inuit used all parts of an animal they killed. They made walrus skin into waterproof boats. Sealskin boots and mittens kept feet and hands warm and dry. They melted snow inside animal bladders for drinking water. To light their homes, the Inuit burned oil made from seal fat.

The Inuit built summer homes from frames made of whale bones that were pushed into the ground. They then covered the bones with caribou skins to make a tent.

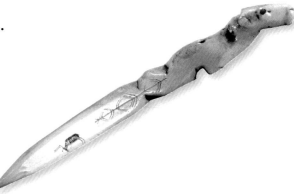

Useful items were made out of small pieces of carved ivory. The handle of this ivory knife was carved to look like an animal head.

Women sometimes used their teeth to pull the needle and thread through the tough sealskin.

Thule Art

The Thule people lived in the Arctic before the Inuit. They were the ancestors of the Inuit.

Thule people made many pieces of art. They carved small ivory statues in the shape of birds or people. The Thule also carved knives, combs, tools, and weapons. They made designs with lines and dots.

Thule statues often had no arms.

11

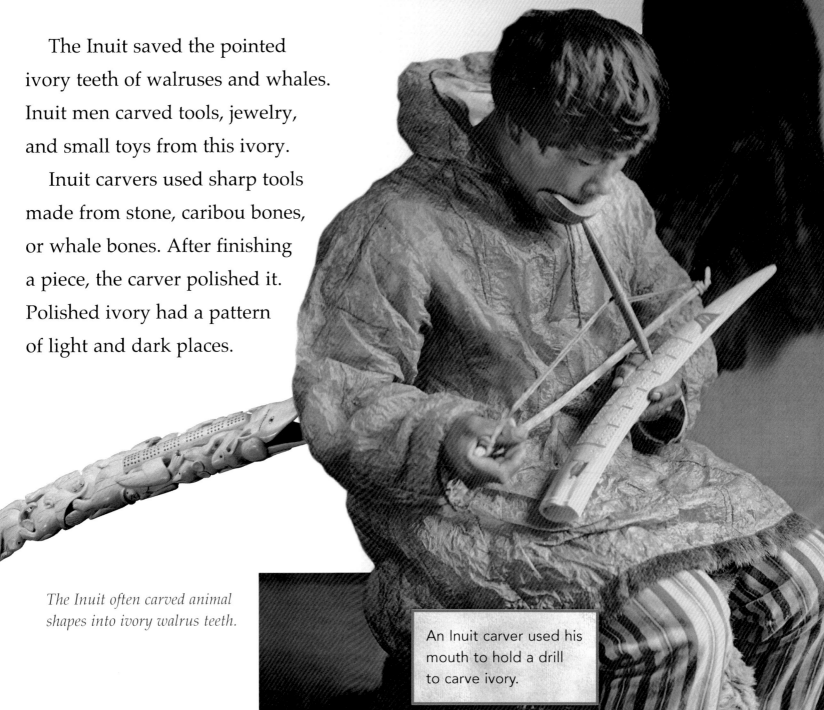

The Inuit saved the pointed ivory teeth of walruses and whales. Inuit men carved tools, jewelry, and small toys from this ivory.

Inuit carvers used sharp tools made from stone, caribou bones, or whale bones. After finishing a piece, the carver polished it. Polished ivory had a pattern of light and dark places.

The Inuit often carved animal shapes into ivory walrus teeth.

An Inuit carver used his mouth to hold a drill to carve ivory.

Make a Soap Carving

Inuit artists often made carvings of animals. They carved polar bears, walruses, caribou, and geese out of ivory. You can practice carving an animal shape from a bar of soap. Be sure to have an adult's help when using a knife to carve.

What You Need

newspaper
bar of bath soap
small paring knife

What You Do

1. Put several layers of newspaper under your work area to catch the soap shavings.
2. Decide what shape you want to carve. It could be a bird, turtle, or other kind of animal.
3. Use the paring knife to scrape away the soap into the shape you have chosen. Carve away from yourself so you do not cut yourself. Do not try to cut the soap or it may splinter or crack.
4. Continue scraping sections of the soap to complete your shape.
5. Use the leftover soap shavings for a bubble bath.

Chapter Four

The Shaman

Ivory carvings and other Inuit artwork sometimes show shamans. The Inuit believed these men and women had magic powers. They believed shamans could cure sick people, control the weather, and see into the future. The Inuit also believed shamans could speak with spirits and change into different animals.

Shamans also searched for lost souls. The Inuit believed that souls could be stolen from people's bodies. They believed if the souls were not returned, those people would die.

Inuit shamans wore sacred masks during some rituals. Here, a shaman is trying to heal a sick boy.

Many Inuit carvings show shamans changing from human form to animal form. This carving shows a shaman changing into a turtle.

Chapter Five

Inuit Storytelling

The Inuit passed down history and lessons through storytelling. Stories often explained how the Inuit should respect the spirits.

Some stories taught the Inuit that animals had souls. The stories gave special rules to show respect to the animals' souls. One way to show respect was to offer a drink of water to a dying animal after a hunt.

Some Inuit stories explained that land animals and sea animals did not belong together. The stories gave rules about keeping sea animals and land animals apart. To follow the rules, the Inuit did not eat seal meat and caribou meat at the same meal. They did not sew walrus skins during caribou season. The Inuit believed if they did not follow the rules, the spirits would send bad luck.

Inuit families cooked, carved, and did other daily chores in their homes. Often, someone told stories to pass the time while everyone worked.

The sea goddess Sedna lived on the bottom of the sea. She watched over the whales, walruses, seals, and fish. She was important in many Inuit stories. Sedna often is shown in Inuit carvings and paintings.

Sedna was an Inuit goddess who protected fish, seals, and other sea animals.

A Crow Brings Daylight

Some Inuit stories explained parts of nature that the Inuit did not understand. This story told why the Arctic had sunlight only in summer.

Long ago, the Inuit saw only darkness. The sky was always dark. Their friend the crow told them about a faraway land where the daytime sky was bright with light. The people begged the crow to bring them this light.

The crow flew in darkness for days. At last, the sky brightened. He saw a small village below him. The crow changed himself into a speck of dust and drifted into the largest igloo.

The village chief sat in the igloo. At his feet, his young son sat playing with toys.

"Ask them for daylight," the crow whispered into the child's ear. The boy said, "Daylight." The boy's father took a small silver ball out of a box. He tied a string to the ball, and the boy pulled the ball outside. Sparks of light shot from the ball.

Once outside, the crow changed back into a bird. He took the string in his beak and carried the silver ball into the air. The crow dropped pieces of light on every Inuit village. But the daylight was heavy. The crow could not carry enough to last all year. For this reason, the far north has six months of darkness and six months of daylight.

Chapter Six

Inuit Clothing and Jewelry

In the Arctic, winter air is so cold it can freeze a person's skin. Even in summer, the air stays cool.

To stay warm, the Inuit wore many layers of clothing made of animal skins. The Inuit invented a hooded coat known as a parka. They sewed parkas out of caribou or walrus skin. The parka's large, fur-lined hood kept the Inuit warm against the cold wind.

The cold Arctic air freezes moisture on a person's hair to form icicles.

The Inuit still wear fur parkas, boots, and gloves to stay warm.

The Inuit also invented snow goggles. When the sun reflected off the snow and ice, its bright rays could blind hunters. The Inuit carved wood or ivory to make goggles with thin slits. These snow goggles protected the Inuit's eyes from bright sunlight.

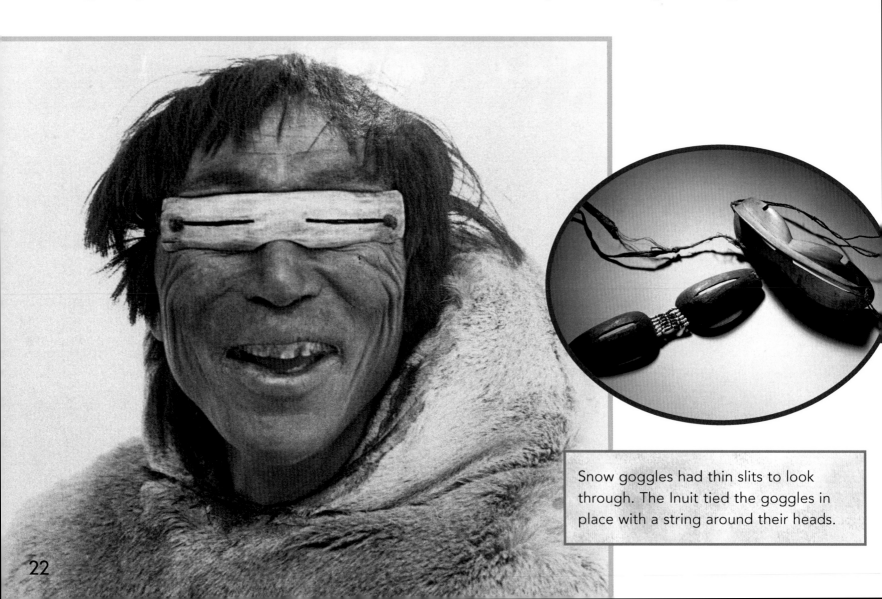

Snow goggles had thin slits to look through. The Inuit tied the goggles in place with a string around their heads.

The Inuit wore jewelry to make their heavy clothing beautiful. They made necklaces with feathers, shells, and pieces of ivory. Inuit women wore hair ornaments made from ivory.

Some Inuit people pierced their noses, ears, and other body parts. At age 12 or 13, many Inuit boys and girls pierced their lower lip. An adult cut a small slit underneath the child's lip. The boys and girls wore ivory lip jewelry in these slits.

The Inuit sometimes wore belts made from shells and ivory over their clothing.

The Inuit often pierced their ears, noses, and lips to wear fancy ivory jewelry.

Chapter Seven

Two Worlds Meet

For many years, the Inuit had few neighbors in the Arctic. They rarely saw other people. The Inuit followed the same ways of hunting and living as they had for many years.

In the 1800s, Inuit life changed when Russian and Canadian whalers came to hunt whales. The Inuit began trading fresh meat and ivory carvings. In exchange, the Inuit received metal tools, knives, and needles. With their new tools, the Inuit began making more detailed carvings.

When foreign whalers came to the Arctic in the 1800s, the Inuit traded food and ivory for new tools.

Kenojuak Ashevak

Kenojuak Ashevak was born in 1927 in an Inuit village. She and her family lived off the land in the same way her ancestors did.

In the 1950s, Ashevak met James Houston. Houston collected Inuit art. With Houston's encouragement, Ashevak began to create drawings and carvings.

Ashevak became a famous Inuit artist. Her art has been featured on three Canadian postage stamps.

In 1948, an artist named James Houston visited an Inuit village. A villager gave him a small carving as a gift. Houston noticed its beauty.

Houston spent many years collecting Inuit carvings. Houston brought his collection to museums. He talked the museums into displaying Inuit carvings.

James Houston, shown with a raven carving, helped Inuit villagers realize the value of their carvings.

In the 19th century, human figures remained popular subjects of Inuit carvings. This carving may have been a shaman's charm.

Inuit Bilboquet

The Inuit played a game called Bilboquet (beel-boh-KAY) with animal bones. The Inuit tied a round, hollow bone onto a long, straight bone with a strip of leather. Inuit players tried to catch the hollow bone with the straight bone. You can make your own version of this Inuit game with a few everyday objects found around the house.

What You Need

a stick

string

a plastic spool (from tape or ribbon)

What You Do

1. Tie the string tightly around one end of the stick.
2. Tie the other end of the string tightly to the plastic spool. (Ask an adult to drill two small holes through the plastic spool. It will be easy to thread the string through the holes and tie it tightly to the spool.)
3. Hold the stick at the end with the string.
4. Flip the spool up and try to catch it with the stick.
5. Keep practicing. See how many times you can catch the spool.

Chapter Eight

The Inuit Today

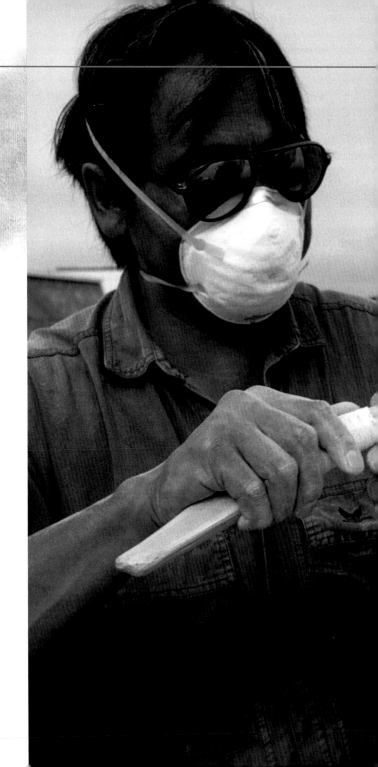

Inuit families still live in the Arctic. They live in wooden houses instead of igloos. Almost every home has a TV. Inuit children attend nearby schools. Many Inuit still hunt for a living. Now they use guns instead of spears.

In 1999, Canada set aside land for the Inuit. The territory was named Nunavut. The name means "our land."

The Inuit are working to keep their traditional way of life. Children learn the Inuit language in school. Many Inuit create ivory or stone carvings. Through art, the Inuit tell the rest of the world about the beauty of the Arctic.

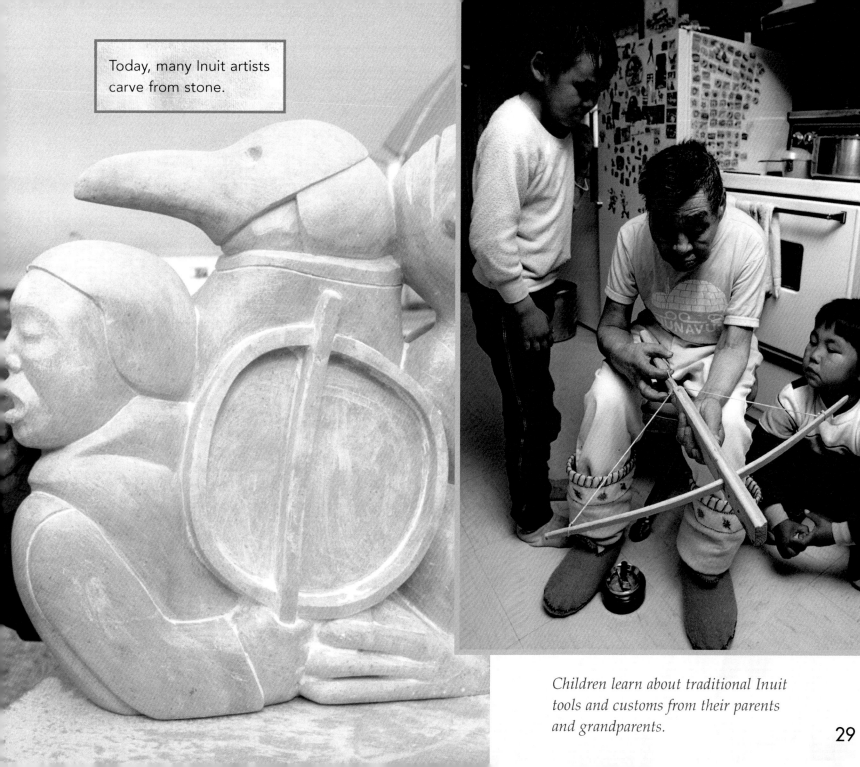

Today, many Inuit artists carve from stone.

Children learn about traditional Inuit tools and customs from their parents and grandparents.

29

Words to Know

Arctic (ARK-tik)—the area near the North Pole

caribou (KA-ri-boo)—a large member of the deer family; caribou have antlers and live mostly in the Arctic.

ivory (EYE-vur-ee)—the natural substance from which the tusks and teeth of some animals are made

kayak (KYE-ak)—a narrow boat with animal-skin bottom and sides

ornament (OR-nuh-muhnt)—a small object used as jewelry or a decoration

shaman (SHAH-muhn)—a religious leader

soul (SOLE)—the part of a living thing that is often thought to control the ability to think, feel, and act

statue (STACH-oo)—a metal, stone, or wood model of a person or an animal

To Learn More

Ansary, Mir Tamim. *Arctic Peoples*. Native Americans. Des Plaines, Ill.: Heinemann Library, 2000.

Corriveau, Danielle. *The Inuit of Canada*. First Peoples. Minneapolis: Lerner, 2002.

Field, Edward. *Magic Words: Poems*. San Diego: Harcourt Brace & Co., 1998.

Finley, Carol. *Art of the Far North: Inuit Sculpture, Drawing, and Printmaking*. Art around the World. Minneapolis: Lerner, 1998.

Lassieur, Allison. *The Inuit*. Native Peoples. Mankato, Minn.: Bridgestone Books, 2000.

Wallace, Mary. *The Inuksuk Book*. Toronto: Owl Books, 1999.

Places to Write and Visit

The Alaska Shop: A Gallery
of Inuit Art
104 East Oak Street
Chicago, IL 60611

McMichael Canadian Art Collection
10365 Islington Avenue
Kleinburg, ON L0J 1C0
Canada

Anchorage Museum of History
and Art
121 West Seventh Avenue
Anchorage, AK 99501

Winnipeg Art Gallery
300 Memorial Boulevard
Winnipeg, MB R3C 1V1
Canada

Internet Sites

Do you want to find out more about the Inuit?
Let FactHound, our fact-finding hound dog, do the research for you.

Here's how:

1) Visit *http://www.facthound.com*
2) Type in the **Book ID** number: **0736821716**
3) Click on **FETCH IT.**

FactHound will fetch Internet sites picked by our editors just for you!

Index